From Marble Mangosteen's Good Deed Collection
Surprising Mrs Rhubarbson

ISBN 978-988-77274-0-8

For more information, please contact the publisher.

Published by:

INSPIRED MUSE!

5/F., Block B, Han Yee Building,
19-21 Hankow Road, Tsim Sha Tsui,
Kowloon, Hong Kong
Email: info@inspiredmusehk.com
Website: www.inspiredmusehk.com

This book is dedicated to
my mother.

TREEBARK VILLAGE
103
A
B
WELCOME

POST OFFICE

Hi, I'm Marble Mangosteen. I live in Treebark Village, Tree 103 A, with my housemate Shooz Starfruiter. Our neighbour, Roxy Rhubarbson, lives downstairs in Tree 103 B. We're all really good friends.

Roxy came upstairs to our house very early this morning. Shooz answered the door. Roxy did not smile. She did not say hello. She just stood there, frowning.

"What happened, Roxy?" asked Shooz.

"It's not fair!" she said.

"What's not fair?" I asked.

"It's Mum," she replied. "It's her birthday today..."

"Then what's not fair?" I asked.

"Mum has to work all day. She'll spend the day at the Old Tree Home looking after everyone. But what about her? I want her to feel special today!" shared Roxy.

"Well... We could help you," I suggested.

Roxy smiled.

"Why don't you join us for breakfast? Here, nibble on some crunchy nuts," Shooz offered.

As we ate breakfast, we all started to think of ideas.

"I know!" said Shooz. "She has a sweet tooth, right? So, let's give her a cake. Maybe it will cheer her up."

"Good idea. We can take it to the Old Tree Home and have a party there! What kind of cake should it be?" Roxy asked.

"Banana!" I shouted.

"And walnuts!" added Shooz.

"With acorn icing!" squealed Roxy. "Perfect!"

"Where can we find this special cake?" Shooz asked.

"Maybe we should try and bake one for her," I suggested. "After all, Mrs Rhubarbson always bakes cakes for us."

"That's true. I always help Mum when she's baking. I think I remember all the steps, but I've never baked by myself. Will both of you help me?" Roxy asked.

"Of course!" we exclaimed.

"I'll bring some bananas," I said. "Shooz can get the nuts and..."

"I'll find the flour and sugar and meet you downstairs," Roxy said.

Shooz scurried to his secret hiding place (which I know is a hole in a tree, by the river near the hospital). I swung to the banana tree behind the post office. I picked the spottiest bunch because they are the sweetest!

The three of us met at Roxy's house. She kept her younger brothers and sisters busy making a birthday card.

We pounded, mashed and stirred everything Roxy told us to. Soon the aroma of cinnamon was swirling through the air.

TING! The timer rang. Roxy put on some gloves and opened the oven door. She carefully took the cake out. We sniffed it and licked our lips.

Shooz, poked it and asked, "How come it's not bouncy?"

"Let's try a small piece," Roxy suggested.

She cut a small slice and divided it into three.

"Mmmmm..." we all said, chewing.

"Maybe it's not a cake," said Shooz. He took another bite. "I think we made a brownie!"

"You're right! I must've remembered the brownie recipe instead." Roxy said.

"But it tastes so good! I'm sure she'll love it!" I said.

Roxy neatly piped “HAPPY BIRTHDAY!” onto the cake with acorn icing. It looked delicious! We carefully put it in a big box and tied a red ribbon on it.

Then Shooz gave a bag to Roxy. She opened it and gasped. Inside were party hats and balloons.

“These were left over from my party last month,” said Shooz. “I thought they might be useful.”

“Thank you,” said Roxy. “They’ll add the finishing touch!”

We blew up the balloons and called Marty Mushroomoni, the Treebark Village mail chimp. He always says:

He sent Garry Grapefruit the giraffe to help us carry everything to the Old Tree Home.

"Please take this, Garry," Roxy said. "And try not to drop it."

"What'shh inside?" asked Garry through closed teeth.

"It's my mum's birthday surprise, a banana and walnut brownie with acorn icing! Come and join us. We're going to the Old Tree Home," Roxy said.

"How hhexciting!" Garry replied as best as he could.

We knocked the door and waited. Nobody answered. We knocked again, louder.

"I'm coming. I'm coming! I only have four paws!" we heard.

When she finally opened the door, we yelled:

"SURPRISE!"

She was speechless. A little tear trickled down her face.

After a long moment, she said, "How thoughtful!"

Inside the Old Tree Home, Eldo Eggington the elephant and Trudy Truffle the turtle were watching the birds outside the window. Olly Okonomiyaki the ostrich was trying to read the newspaper, which was a bit tricky without his glasses.

Mrs. Rhubarbson was delighted! The residents of the Old Tree Home felt special too.

"Is that cinnamon?" asked Eldo, sniffing the box.

I snapped pictures as we lit candles on the brownie. Olly started singing the "Happy Birthday" song and we all joined in with Trudy clapping away. Everyone cheered and laughed merrily.

DING DONG! The doorbell rang.

It was Nathan and Nancy Noodle the nightingales. Behind them were Wendy and Walter Waffle the weasels. Then came Bernie and Brenda Breadson the bears.

"We heard Olly singing," said Bernie.

"Happy Birthday!" they all wished Mrs Rhubarbson.

The animals at the Old Tree Home told us how much our visit had brightened their day. The bears, weasels and nightingales asked if they could come back and work there. As for Mrs Rhubarbson, she said it was the happiest birthday she'd ever had. She loved our surprise!

8 May 2016

Dear Diary,

They LOVED the brownie! And the party! And EVERYTHING! They were so happy! I've never seen them smile so much!

Especially Mrs Rhubarbson. She gave Roxy a hug and said she was so proud of her and all the rest of us!

After the party, Roxy, Shooz and I decided to make this a regular thing. We're going to start a new collection of fruit and nuts so that we can visit and have a party at the Old Tree Home every month!

Everyone there is excited about this. They're planning games and a theme for the next party already!

Marty has also agreed to send out invitations to everyone in Treebark Village for free.

I have to sleep now. The three of us are going to meet early tomorrow to start collecting fruit and nuts for next month!

Good night!
Marble

Write a diary about something good you did for someone else and draw a picture to go with it.

Discussion Points

To help answer questions about the story, readers can use their personal experiences.

Q1. Who are the four main characters?
Q2. Why is Roxy upset at the beginning?
Q3. What do they make for Mrs Rhubarbson and where do they go?
Q4. How does Mrs Rhubarbson feel about her surprise?
Q5. Why do they decide to make what they make?
Q6. Can you find three kind acts in this book? Why are they kind?
Q7. What do you do when it's a grown-up's birthday?
Q8. Can you think of other ways to surprise someone?
Q9. Why do you think the animals at the Old Tree Home are happy when Marble, Shooz, Roxy and everyone else come to visit?
Q10. If your friend asks you for help, how would you respond?

Discussion Point Explanations

E1. The four main characters are Marble Mangosteen (the monkey), Shooz Starfruiter (the squirrel), Roxy Rhubarbson and her mum, Mrs Rhubarbson (the racoons).

E2. Roxy is upset because she doesn't want her mum to spend her birthday working alone. She wants to make the day special for her.

E3. They made a banana and walnut brownie with acorn icing and took it to the Old Tree Home to surprise Mrs Rhubarbson.

E4. Mrs Rhubarbson feels surprised and touched that the children remembered her birthday and wanted her to feel special.

E5. They decided to bake a cake because Mrs Rhubarbson always bakes cakes for them and because she has a sweet tooth.

E6. The story has many, but here are three:

- Marble chooses the spottiest banana bunch because they are the sweetest and Mrs Rhubarbson likes sweet things.
- The children want to surprise Mrs Rhubarbson to show her that she is special too.
- The children spent time with the people at the Old Tree Home by giving them company.

E7. Wish them Happy Birthday and make them feel special by getting or making them something (e.g. a card or a present).

E8. Do a performance, make an art and craft project or pamper the person (e.g. give them a massage).

E9. The animals at the Old Tree Home were happy because they must have enjoyed the company. Olly got a chance to sing (which was one of his hobbies). Before that, he was bored trying to read the newspaper without his glasses.

E10. I would try to see if I could help my friend and we would work together to solve the problem, or we would try to get help from someone else.

Noun Glossary

acorn – a nut that comes from an oak tree

chimp – short for chimpanzee (a species of great ape. They have no tails.)

cinnamon – a spice usually used in foods like apple pie

grapefruit – a fruit that looks like an orange but is more bitter

mangosteen – a purplish fruit (found in Asia) with white flesh in the centre

nightingale – a beautiful bird with a lovely voice

okonomiyaki – a Japanese pancake

ostrich – a large bird that can't fly

racoon – (also spelled as raccoon) a fox-like animal with greyish brown fur

rhubarb – a red-coloured vegetable but is often used in pies and tarts

squirrel – a bushy-tailed rodent that lives in trees all around the world except Australia and Antarctica

starfruit – a special fruit that looks like a star when it's cut down its short side

truffle – a food that grows underground, similar to a mushroom

About the Author

Reena Bhojwani was born and brought up in Hong Kong. She graduated from the University of Melbourne with a degree in Creative Arts. She has been teaching creative writing to children in Hong Kong for over 6 years. She enjoys bringing out the best in them. Reena also serves as an active member of the Hong Kong Writers Circle. In her free time, she enjoys reading, playing board games, dancing and having fun with her family and friends.

Printed in Great Britain
by Amazon

34480944R00021